THE RENAISSANCE

Published by
UNIVERSITY SCHOOL
at The University of Tulsa

TULSA, OKLAHOMA

© 1998 University School
First Edition, 1998. Reprinted 2007.
All rights reserved. Individual teachers who purchase this book are welcome to make copies for their own classes. Entire schools and districts who wish to use the series may purchase books at bulk rate. Making copies from one book for multiple classrooms or schools is prohibited.

ISBN Number: 1-893413-02-0

Manufactured in the United States of America

All proceeds from this series go to University School at The University of Tulsa, a non-profit educational organization.

SAILS titles include:
- *Classical Greece*
- *Ancient Rome*
- *The Renaissance*
- *Baroque & Rococo*
- *Neoclassicism*
- *Romanticism*
- *Ancient Egypt*
- *Middle Ages*

Other books are in the planning phase. Additional information is available about SAILS materials and University School.

Contact: University School at The University of Tulsa
600 South College Avenue, Tulsa, Oklahoma 74104
Phone: 918-631-5060   Fax: 918-631-5065
Visit: 326 South College Avenue, Tulsa, Oklahoma 74104
e-mail: debra-price@utulsa.edu

The University of Tulsa is an equal opportunity/affirmative action institution. For EEO/AA information, contact the Office of Legal Compliance at (918) 631-2423, for disability accommodations, contact Dr. Jane Corso at (918) 631-2315.

The SAILS Curriculum concept and ideas were developed in conjunction with a grant from the U.S. Department of Education, Javits Gifted and Talented Students Education Grants Program; Award Number R206A990007 for the period January 1999 through January 2003; in the amount of $645,000.

Acknowledgements

Many thanks to Susan Coman and her staff at Protype Inc., Tulsa, Oklahoma, who produced the series. Also thanks to copy editors Katie Abercrombie, Robyn Bowman, Ekta Gupta, Kim Harper, and Andrea Sharrer for the countless hours donated to this project.

Artwork courtesy of Photodisc, Artchives, clip art, and Patricia Hollingworth. Any omission of acknowledgement is unintentional.

Students' Active Interdisciplinary Learning Series

Preface

University School teachers created SAILS for students of all ages. SAILS is based on active interdisciplinary learning in a content-rich environment as used at University School. University School at The University of Tulsa is a school for gifted children from preschool through eighth grade. The active interdisciplinary learning approach presented in SAILS enables gifted behaviors to emerge in students in both regular and special classrooms.

The purpose of SAILS is to provide a framework for understanding historical patterns which is often omitted in world, national, and art history courses. This framework is developed by showing modern day links to ancient Western civilizations, presenting reccurring patterns in history, and acquiring an understanding of the basic ideals of these cultures. Every community in America has visual reminders of ancient civilizations which go unrecognized. Students of all ages can learn to recognize and appreciate this heritage.

SAILS was created by

Editor and Illustrator - Patricia L. Hollingsworth, Ed.D.

Writers and Teachers

Katie Abercrombie	Marilyn Howard
Sharon Block	Cyndie Kidwell
Debi Foster	Gina Lewis
Cathy Freeman	Alicia Parent
Kim Harper	Marti Sudduth

Patricia Hollingsworth

Contents

TIMELINE / 6

INTRODUCTION

    Introduction by Michelangelo..9
    Quick Facts...12

IDEALS

    Just Before the Renaissance..16
    Middle Ages Questions..17
    Renaissance..18
    Middle Ages and Renaissance Comparison.......................................19
    The 1300s..20
    The 1400s..21
    Renaissance Activity..23

DAILY LIFE

    Is This Your Room?...24
    Clothing for Males...25
    Clothing for Females...26
    Renaissance Clothing..27
    Sights, Sounds, and Smells...28

ARTISTS

    Donatello...29
    Profile Portraits..32
    Botticelli...33
    La Primavera..34
    Raphael..38
    Connections to the Past..41
    Stories in Picture..42

RENAISSANCE MEN: LEONARDO, DÜRER, MICHAELANGELO

    Leonardo da Vinci: Artist and Scientist...44
    Leonardo's Parachute..45
    Mona Lisa..46
    Albrectht Dürer: Artist and Scientist..47
    Dürer's Rabbit..51
    Michelangelo's Studio...53
    Michalangelo..55
    Michelangelo the Sculptor...56
    Michelangelo the Painter...57
    Michelangelo the Architect..58
    Michelangelo's Assistant..59

ARCHITECTS
    Brunelleschi's Dome 60
    Palladio 62
    Michelangelo 63

WRITERS/MUSIC
    Renasissance Music 64
    Musical Activity 65
    Ben Jonson 67
    William Shakespeare 70

SCIENCE & MATH
    Arch and Lintel Experiments 77
    Renaissance Dome 79
    Make Concrete 80
    Experiment with Printing 82
    Magnifying the World 83
    Lead Pencils 84
    Observe the Natural World 85
    Renaissance of Numbers 89
    Math Signs 92
    Crossword 94
    Napier's Bones 96
    Inventor Match 99

EXPLORATION
    Renaissance Explorers 100
    Henry the Navigator 101
    Columbus 102
    You are a Sailor with Columbus 104
    Explorers and Inventions Activity 107

REVIEW
    Evaluation 109
    Letters Home 110

BIBLIOGRAPHY / 111

TIME LINE

This timeline is a simplified version of time periods. The dates are all approximate and in reality overlap with one another. One country may be starting a time period just as another is ending it. The idea is to provide some guidelines for understanding ideas and influences.

	800BC-350AD	**350-1350AD**	**1350-1600AD**
	CLASSICAL • GREEK • ROMAN	**MEDIEVAL/MIDDLE AGES** • ROMANESQUE • GOTHIC	**RENAISSANCE**

IDEALS

- **Classical Greek Ideals:**
  Freedom
  Symmetry
  Balance
  Beauty
  Order
  Dignity
  "Nothing to excess"

- **Classical Roman Ideals:**
  Grandeur
  Power
  Efficiency
  Practicality

- Life is short, difficult
- God all important
- Afterlife all important

- **Classical Ideals Revived:**
  God and humans important
  Harmony
  Balance
  Beauty
  Order
  Grandeur
  Power

ARCHITECTURE

- **Greek Classical:**
  Parthenon
  Balance, harmony, order

- **Roman Classical:**
  Pantheon
  Technology advancements

- **Romanesque:**
  Fortress-like

- **Gothic:**
  God-like proportion
  Light, airy
  Spires point to God

- **Renaissance Classical:**
  Symmetrical
  Built for God and humans
  Human proportions
  Solid

ART

- **Greeks: Idealistic**
  Classical ideals
- **Romans: Realistic**
  Mythological and
    human subjects
  Classical ideals

- Stiff, heavily draped sculpture
- Cartoon-like drawings
- Biblical subjects only

- Natural and realistic
- Balanced between repose and action
- Biblical, mythological, and human subjects

1600-1750AD	1750-1800AD	1800-1850AD
• BAROQUE • ROCOCO	NEOCLASSICAL	ROMANTIC

IDEALS

- **Baroque**
  Emotion
  Grandeur
  Energy

- **Rococo**
  Enjoyment
  Pleasure

- **Classical Ideals Revived:**
  Freedom
  Dignity
  Balance
  Beauty
  Order

- Emotion
- Imagination
- Freedom
- Energy
- Turbulence

ARCHITECTURE

- **Versailles:**
  Elaborate
  Grand
- **Palaces:**
  Ornate
  Gold leaf
  Curlicues

- **Monticello:**
  Symmetry
  Balance
  Solid

- **Parliament Houses:**
  Gothic and Medieval

ART

- **Baroque:**
  Emotional
  Swirling
  Dramatic Subject Lighting
- **Rococo:**
  Pretty and Pleasant

- **Classical Ideals:**
  Balance
  Harmony
  Dignity

- Emotional
- Swirling
- Dramatic and exotic
  Lighting
  Subjects

THE RENAISSANCE

1350-1600 AD

Welcome to the Renaissance

INTRO

My name is Michelangelo. Most people remember me for painting the Sistine Chapel, which I never wanted to do. I did not even want to paint. Sculpture is my real strength, but I am also an architect. I tried to get the architect Palladio to come with me, but he is busy designing a building based on the Roman Pantheon.

The Renaissance was a rebirth of classical Greek and Roman ideals, art, literature, and architecture. Architects again placed an emphasis on balance, symmetry, and human proportions as in the days of the classical Greeks and Romans. During the end of the Medieval Era, or Middle Ages, Gothic churches looked like lace. They were complex to look at, but also had an airy feel.

Michelangelo

Stiff Medieval Art

Classic Renaissance Architecture

INTRO

Michelangelo

During the Renaissance we made buildings simpler and more solid. Buildings used features from the classical world, such as Greek pediments and columns and Roman arches and domes. After years of complex and ornate Gothic cathedrals with their stiff, heavily draped sculpture, people were ready for something new. I will show you an example of my sculpture when you come to my studio later.

I cannot tell you what a breath of fresh air the Renaissance was for those of us in Florence. It was almost as if the human spirit had been dead for the 1,000 years of the Middle Ages. No wonder they sometimes call them "Dark Ages". There had been wars, raids, hunger, pestilence, plague, and constant fear. The Renaissance was a rebirth of our God-given human spirit.

MICHELANGELO'S RENAISSANCE INTRODUCTION

INTRO

1. Occupations that Michelangelo liked: _____ _____

2. Something he was good at but did not like to do: _____

3. The time period just before the Renaissance: _____

4. Renaissance means: _____

5. Renaissance was a return to: _____

6. Architects placed emphasis on: _____

7. Gothic architecture was: _____ _____

8. Renaissance buildings were: _____ _____

9. Architectural features borrowed from classical Greeks: _____

    and _____

10. Architectural features borrowed from classical Romans: _____

    and _____

11. Name of the chapel in Rome that Michelangelo painted: _____

12. Name two important cities during the Renaissance: _____

Renaissance WORDBOX

rebirth	dome	Florence and Rome
Sistine	pediment	balance, symmetry, and
sculptor	columns	human proportion
architect	light and complex	Medieval, Middle Ages,
arch	solid and simple	Dark Ages
painting	classical Greek and Roman	

RENAISSANCE
QUICK FACTS

1350-1600 AD

Medieval Life

Time Period Just Prior To Renaissance

- Medieval Era, Middle Ages, Dark Ages, circa 350-1350 AD
- A time of wars, raids, famine, fear, plague
- Lasted about 1,000 years

Dates - circa (meaning about) 1350 — 1600 AD

- As with any time period, dates are approximate. The Renaissance began and ended at different times in different countries.

Values & Ideals

- Belief that human spirit and creativity were divinely inspired
- Revival of classical Greek and Roman ideals and values
- Renewed interest in mythology, often combined with Biblical stories
- Naturalism, simplicity, balance, individualism
- Renewed interest in human beings and life on earth
- Renewed interest in science, biology, anatomy
- Awakening interest in exploring and inventing

Foremost Cities

- Florence — ruled by plutocrat family, the Medici
  Rome
- Venice — ruled by wealthy oligarchy

Famous People

- 1276-1337 — Giotto, artist
- 1304-1374 — Petrarch, poet
- 1401-1428 — Masaccio (ma SAHT chee oh), painter, famous for using light and shadows

Classical Greek Art

- 1386-1466 — Donatello, sculptor
- 1445-1510 — Botticelli, painter
- 1452-1519 — Leonardo da Vinci, painter, inventor, architect
- 1475-1564 — Michelangelo, sculptor, painter, architect
- 1483-1520 — Raphael, painter
- 1471-1528 — Albrecht Dürer, painter, engraver

Science

- 1473-1543 — Copernicus, Polish astronomer, theory that Earth moves
- 1564-1642 — Galileo, perfected telescope to prove Copernicus' theory

Renaissance Life

Explorations

- 1418 — Prince Henry, sailing expeditions
- 1492 — Columbus
- 1519 — Cortez

Inventions

- 1450 — Gutenberg, moveable type and printing press
- 1450 — Nicholas of Cusa, concave lense for nearsighted
- 1500 — Peter Henlein, portable clock
- 1565 — Konrad von Gesner, pencil
- 1568 — Jacques Besson, first screw cutting lathe
- 1569 — Mercator, new projector or map making (cartography)
- 1589 — William Lee, knitting machine
- 1590 — Hans Jensen, compound microscope
- 1590 — Hans Lippershey, telescope
- 1592 — Galileo, thermometer
- 1594 — John Napier, logarithms

Others

- navigational instruments — such as astrolabe
- etching
- oil painting
- paper money and bank notes
- accurate mechanical clocks
- the merchant class leading to middle class

Prince Henry the Navigator

QUICK FACTS

- wooden screws
- grenades
- the pistol
- the shirt

Artists

- used oil painting more than egg tempera or fresco
- used light and shadow called *chiaroscuro* (key arrow SKEWR o)
- studied anatomy, used natural poses, used s-curve
- discovered laws of perspective
- used lifelike colors
- used deeper space

Scientists

- artists were often scientists (Brunelleschi, Leonardo, Dürer)
- studied biology, botany, and anatomy
- involved in inventions
- interested in exploration and discoveries

Architecture

- return to classical architecture
- columns, pediments, domes
- simpler, more solid looking, using human proportions
- Brunelleschi (brew nell LESS kee) dome in Florence
- Palladio, Villa Rotonda
- Michelangelo, dome of St. Peter's Cathedral

Classical Architecture with Pediment and Columns

Activity~

RENAISSANCE TRIVIAL PURSUIT

1. What are the approximate dates of the Renaissance? _____

2. Name five famous Renaissance artists: _____
   _____

3. Write the artistic term meaning light and shadow: _____
   _____

4. What were some of the ideals of the Renaissance? _____
   _____
   _____

5. What were some of the discoveries or inventions during the Renaissance?

6. Name of the banking family that ruled Florence? _____

7. Name two explorers: _____

8. Name a poet: _____

9. Who invented the thermometer? _____

10. Who invented the printing press? _____

11. Name three people who were both artists and scientists: _____
    _____

12. What was new in art? _____

15

RENAISSANCE IDEALS

JUST BEFORE THE RENAISSANCE

Middle Ages or Medieval Era

During the 1,000 years of the Middle Ages, life seemed particularly fragile. People focused on the afterlife in the face of imminent death. It was a time of war, ignorance, superstition, and fear. People did not expect to live long, and the life they had was often full of toil and suffering. Most of the people were peasants who worked for a noble in exchange for some protection in time of war. This was known as feudalism. There was little trade, and the economy was based on what the noble's estate could produce. A bad harvest could mean ruin.

Medieval Sculpture

In addition to difficult economic times, during the Middle Ages war was a fact of life. The nobles warred among themselves, and barbaric tribes invaded all of Europe. To see the prow of a Nordic ship sailing in a nearby river meant almost certain death. Barbarian was the name given to the wild and savage tribes that roamed Europe during the Dark Ages. It was a time of death, disease, and daily drudgery.

During the Medieval era, art was only done for the church. People lived short and dreary lives. Their hopes for anything better were not on earth but in heaven. The art was often done in a stern, stiff manner. Unlike the classical Greeks and Romans, the drapery of the Medieval sculpture hid the human figure with long stiff lines.

Medieval Life

Activity~

IDEALS

Middle Ages Questions

The Middle Ages lasted about _____ years.

Most people were _____.

Working as a peasant for a noble was called _____.

Art was done for the _____.

Most people hopes were for _____.

The tribes who invaded Europe were called _____.

Make a list of many and varied single words to describe the Middle Ages.

_____

_____

_____

_____

_____

Use your answers from above in the grid to create your own crossword puzzle.

RENAISSANCE

WORD**BOX**

barbarian	church
peasants	drudgery
feudalism	ignorance
heaven	

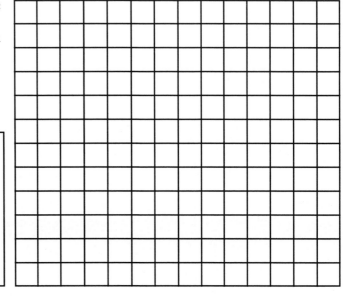

17

IDEALS

The Renaissance

Renaissance City

Renaissance means rebirth. It meant a new interest in the values and ideals of the classical Greeks and Romans as well as a new interest in this world rather than the afterlife. It was a time of renewed interest in the world and all that it held. Humans were seen as God's ultimate creation. It was, therefore, the duty of humans to learn all they could and become all they could be.

The Renaissance which followed the Medieval time period (Middle Ages) occurred in part because capitalism replaced feudalism. This meant that people had other options than just working as peasants in exchange for a noble's protection (feudalism).

In the city of Florence, it meant there were jobs in trade. There were wool and silk merchants, craftsmen, and bankers. During the crusades, Florentines had made money through wool and banking. They proudly remembered their history as being part of the Roman Empire. Italy was becoming a major trade center. Many of the peasant class were joining the middle class.

In Florence groups of people met to discuss art, politics, music, and literature. They called the groups Plato's Academy. Renaissance artists often use a Greek and Roman mythology as a theme along with Biblical stories. The people of Florence loved anything from the classical past.

Dürer's Angels

Renaissance Academy

18

Middle Ages & Renaissance Comparison

Compare these two time periods in as many ways as possible. Use the information from the previous page and the the IDEA BOX to help you.

IDEALS

	THE MIDDLE AGES	THE RENAISSANCE
ART		
ECONOMY		
JOBS		
INTERESTS		
ATTITUDES		
INVENTIONS		
DISCOVERIES		
ARCHITECTURE		
LIFE STYLE		
OTHER		

Renaissance

WORD BOX

ignorant	educated	peasant	mythology
feudalism	capitalism	barbarian	human
Renaissance	rebirth	Medieval	individual
Florence	merchant	heaven	trade

19

Early Renaissance

Painter Giotto's artwork

Petrarch

THE 1300s IN FLORENCE

The painter **Giotto** (ZHOTT-o) was born around 1267 and died in 1337. He did frescoes for the church which were more natural and realistic than those done during the Middle Ages. Frescoes are wall paintings in which paint is added to wet plaster. Giotto also made his figures look like individuals with human feelings, unlike the stiff, stern figures of the Medieval period. It was said that his work looked so naturalistic that his teacher tried to brush a fly away from Giotto's painting only to discover that it was part of the painting. One of his famous paintings is *St. Francis Preaching to the Birds*.

Petrarch (1304-1374) encouraged people to read and discuss the literature from the Greeks and Romans. This revived interest in reading the classics in the original Greek and Latin in which they had been written. Petrarch wrote in his own language and encouraged others to do the same. He wrote a series of sonnets (love poems) to his cherished Laura, which poets used as models for hundreds of years.

Activity~

IDEALS

Fill out an imaginary job application for these men.

Name: Petrarch

Date of Birth: _____

Home City: _____

Seek job as: _____

Experience: _____

Hobbies: _____

Reasons you should be hired: _____

_____

_____

_____

_____

Name: Giotto

Date of Birth: _____

Home City: _____

Seek job as: _____

Experience: _____

Hobbies: _____

Reasons you should be hired: _____

_____

_____

_____

_____

THE 1400s IN FLORENCE

In the 1400s artists began to discover the laws of perspective and began to use oil paints. Both of these discoveries contributed to the advances that painting made during the Renaissance. Both oil paints and perspective made it possible for artists to create greater realism than ever.

Masaccio (ma-SAHT-chee-o), also a Florentine, was born in 1401 and only lived to be 27. In his short life he accomplished much. Following Giotto's lead, he created even more solid and realistic figures, used accurate perspective and used *chiaroscuro* (key-arrow-SKEWR-o), a technique of light and shadow. One of his most famous works is *The Tribute Money*.

Masaccio's painting

Donatello (1386-1466), contrary to what you may have heard, was a sculptor from Florence. His *David* was the first life-sized, free-standing sculpture since the time of the classical Greeks and Romans. Donatello used *contrapposto*, which is the natural looking pose with the body weight on one leg and the other leg bent. This produces a natural looking "s-curve" shape to the body. During the Renaissance, artists were again looking at the human body as a thing of beauty, just as they had in classical times.

Donatello's *David*

IDEALS

Activity~

IDEALS

Fill out an imaginary job application for these men.

Name: Donatello

Date of Birth: _____

Home City: _____

Seek job as: _____

Experience: _____

Hobbies: _____

Reasons you should be hired: _____

_____

_____

_____

_____

Name: Masaccio

Date of Birth: _____

Home City: _____

Seek job as: _____

Experience: _____

Hobbies: _____

Reasons you should be hired: _____

_____

_____

_____

_____

RENAISSANCE
DAILY LIFE

Is This Your Room?

COMPARE AND CONTRAST

If you lived in Renaissance Florence, your bedroom might have had a massive bed with intricate carvings, an elaborate canopy, and rich drapes. The bed might have stood on an imported carpet. You might have kept mulberry twigs under the bed because they attracted fleas from the double mattresses on your bed. A colorful tapestry might hang on your wall.

Does this sound like your bedroom? Draw two pictures below, one illustrating the Renaissance bedroom and the other illustrating your bedroom at home.

List two things that are similar in the two bedrooms.

1. _____

2. _____

List two things that are different about the two bedrooms.

3. _____

4. _____

Renaissance Clothing for Males

The clothing of Renaissance times was colorful and elaborate. The business of dying and finishing woven fabrics was in full swing.

Men still wore the short tunics as the Romans did, but now the tunics were brightly colored. A man or boy might wear a bright blue tunic with red tights. They wore soft leather boots and simple caps on their heads.

On the left is a drawing of a young boy in Renaissance clothing. Draw a picture of a young boy in modern clothing in the box.

Renaissance Man

DAILY LIFE

Renaissance Boy

Did you know that Renaissance people would hide a piece of fur somewhere on their bodies. They did this so that lice would be attracted to the fur instead of to them!

Renaissance Clothing for Females

DAILY LIFE

Women of the Renaissance did not wear tunics. They wore full, flowing dresses with tight bodices and high necklines. They also wore high platform shoes. These shoes helped them cross muddy streets without getting the hem of their dresses dirty.

Design a Renaissance dress of your own:

Renaissance Woman

Renaissance Woman

Stylish Renaissance women plucked their foreheads to make them appear higher. They also bleached and frizzed their hair.

26

Renaissance Clothing

Use a whole sheet of paper to design some Renaissance clothing of your own. Here are some pictures of Renaissance people to use as examples. Be creative and think about what you would have liked if you were a Renaissance citizen.

DAILY LIFE

Renaissance Young People

Sights, Sounds and Smells of Renaissance Florence

Everything listed below was common in Renaissance Florence. Pretend you are walking through Florence and imagine what it was like. Imagine how things looked, felt, sounded, and smelled. Circle in red all the things that are similiar to where you live. Circle in green all of the things that are not.

Renaissance City

City gates that open at dawn

Farmers with donkey carts

Narrow, paved streets

Stonecutters

Bankers

Artists' street

Grocers

Chickens

Garbage

Hot

Construction workers

Evening curfew

Goldsmiths

Marble workers

Fishmongers

Butchers

Fish

Horses

Sewage

Humid

Merchants

Blacksmiths

Cabinet makers

Jewelers

RENAISSANCE ARTISTS

Habbakuk

Donatello
1386-1466

The first half of the fifteenth century is known as the early Renaissance. During the Middle Ages, artwork had mostly been created for the glory of God, not for the glory of the artist or the artwork itself. Attitudes about art and artists began to change at the beginning of the Renaissance. People began to think of artists not as lowly craftsmen, but as creative people who were to be appreciated. Nowhere did the change come about more quickly than in the city of Florence in Italy.

One of the greatest sculptors of this time was Donatello. Donatello di Niccolo Bardi was born in Florence in 1386. When he was a teenager, he became an apprentice to the sculptor Lorenzo Ghiberti. Becoming an apprentice meant that in exchange for learning a craft or trade, a student would do work for his teacher. Donatello probably worked around Ghiberti's studio, doing odd jobs at first, and then progressed to actually working with sculpture.

ARTISTS

When he was only 29, Donatello's talents began to match those of his teacher. He carved a marble statue of St. George and a relief *St. George Killing The Dragon*. A relief is a carved or modeled art work in which the figures project out from the background. In the statue of St. George, the subject looks relaxed and appears to be deep in thought. This work of art is very important because this was the first statue constructed since ancient times that could actually stand by itself. In addition Donatello was the first to show a statue with its clothing as a secondary part of the body. In other words a viewer can see the shape of St. George's body under his clothing and armor.

Eight years later Donatello carved an unusual statue of the prophet *Habbakuk*.

Donatello's *David*

The statue was nicknamed "Zuccone," or in English, "Pumpkinhead." This prophet was not noble or beautiful, but as the nickname implies, ugly and strange looking. This was his first piece of work to carry his signature, so we know Donatello must have been proud of it.

Donatello worked not only in marble, but also in bronze. In the 1420s, he made a full-sized bronze statue of *David*. Again, this statue was important for it was the first freestanding statue to portray a life-sized male form since ancient times. In fact *David* was the only statue of this kind to be produced for many years. Donatello would go on to create two more bronze statues of David. In the 1430s his statue of David was done in a distinctly classical style, as if Donatello was influenced by ancient Greek and Roman artists.

In 1443 Donatello was invited to the city of Padua to cast in bronze a statue of the commander of the Venetian army. This statue, the artist's largest freestanding work in bronze, still stands on a pedestal near a church where Donatello directed it to be placed more than 550 years ago. The statue is of a horse and a rider dressed in full armor. The horse is looking to one side, and its left front leg is mounted daintily upon a small sphere. The horse looks strong and powerful, and its rider looks comfortable and at ease. The statue, which took many years to complete, is thirteen feet long and eleven feet high.

Donatello's sculptures, both beautiful and naturalistic, affected sculptors throughout Italy and the rest of Europe, not only during the time in which Donatello lived, but through the ages to today.

Donatello lived to be a very old man. He produced art work all of his life; his statue of the Venetian commander was completed when he was in his 70s! Donatello died in 1466 at the age of 80.

Donatello's Equestrian Statue

Donatello True or False

Mark each of the following statements either T for true or F for false. If a statement is false, rewrite it to make it a true statement.

_____ The first half of the fifteenth century is known as the high Renaissance.

_____ During the Middle Ages, artwork was created for the glory of God.

_____ Donatello was born in Florence in 1386.

_____ An apprentice receives nothing for working for an artist.

_____ Donatello became an apprentice to Lorenzo Ghiberti.

_____ Donatello was only 29 when people began to notice his talents.

_____ A relief is a kind of carving that tells a story.

_____ "Pumpkinhead" is a statue the artist created of himself.

_____ Donatello signed "Pumpkinhead."

_____ Donatello sculpted one statue of David.

_____ Donatello's statue of the Venetian commander was destroyed in a war.

_____ Donatello created statues from marble and bronze.

ARTISTS

Donatello's *Penitent Magdalene*

Renaissance Profiles

The new interest in the lives of people on earth, as opposed to the otherworldly interests of the Middle Ages, led to a great many portraits being painted during the Renaissance. One early Renaissance style was the profile portrait. Roman coins with profiles on them may have been the inspiration for the profile portrait. The profile of the person is large and in the foreground. In the background is a landscape that appears to recede almost endlessly.

Paolo Uccello's (1397-1475) profile portrait is of a young man. This handsome young Renaissance man was probably knowledgable about Greek and Roman ideals, curious about the world, successful in his career, and confident about his future. This young man seems to typify the Renaissance man.

The profile portrait by **Piero della Francesco** (1420-1492) shows absolute realism and nobility at the same time. The profile is of Federigo da Montefeltro, whose face had been disfigured by a sword in a tournament. The man had lost one eye and the bridge of his nose. Yet his head is held high, as if he refused to let the trauma ruin his life.

Portrait of a Young Woman painted by **Antonio del Pollaiuolo** (1432-1498) in the 1460s is another example of a Renaissance profile. Though the woman's name is unknown, there are things we can surmise from the portrait. She appears to be a refined, wealthy, and capable young woman.

Draw profile portraits of three different people:

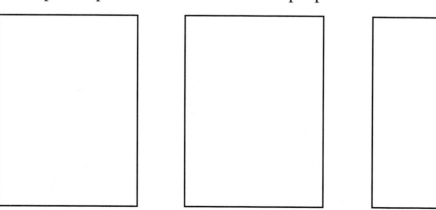

Sandro Botticelli
ca. 1445-1510

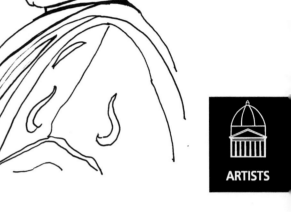

Florentine painter Sandro Botticelli's (circa 1445-1510) portrait of a young man is not in absolute profile. It is more like the three-quarter style of portraits that became popular in the 1470s.

What do you imagine this young man is like? Would you want to know him? Why do you suppose Botticelli painted him?

Look at the self-portrait of Botticelli. What do you think it tells about him? Now, using a mirror, draw your own self-portrait.

Portrait by Botticelli

LA PRIMAVERA

Botticelli's Self Portrait

Botticelli is best known for his mythological works such as *La Primavera* (Spring) and *Birth of Venus*. His figures are graceful and his colors beautiful. The highly idealized beauty in his work holds a spiritual quality.

The setting for *La Primavera* is an orange grove heavily laden with fruit. On the far right, the wind god Zephyrus turns a nymph into Flora, goddess of spring. This is why flowers are coming from her mouth. The calm, beautiful woman standing next to her is the person she becomes when she is completely transformed into Flora. The now fully formed Flora, goddess of spring, is throwing flowers upon the grass, from her lovely, flower-covered dress.

On the far left, we see Mercury idly waiting. He looks much like Donatello's statue of David. Perhaps he is guarding the group or waiting to deliver a message. The three graces dance to his right while the blindfolded Cupid shoots golden arrows in their direction. In Greek mythology the Three Graces are Zeus's daughters Joy, Bloom, and Brilliance. They are the goddesses of musical and artistic talents.

The lovely lady in the middle is Venus dressed as a Florentine married woman. She is wearing the headdress that married women in Florence wore.

Goddess Flora
from *La Primavera*

Activity~

1. Look at Botticelli's *La Primavera* on page 36. Imagine coming across these gods and goddesses in the woods. Now record what you would:

SEE	HEAR	TOUCH	SMELL	TASTE

ARTISTS

2. Use these ideas to describe what Botticelli's painting tells you about spring.

_____
_____
_____
_____
_____
_____
_____
_____
_____
_____

Observing Things

LET'S REALLY LOOK AT A PAINTING

Study Botticelli's painting *La Primavera* carefully and then answer the following questions.

Bottiicelli's *La Primavera*

1. **Subjects** — check what you see

   ❏ animals ❏ buildings ❏ trees ❏ children

   ❏ flowers ❏ adults ❏ musical instruments

   ❏ indoors ❏ outdoors ❏ transportation vehicles

   ❏ sky ❏ food ❏ other

2. **Lines** — check what you see

   ❏ sharp ❏ curved ❏ choppy ❏ thick

   ❏ thin ❏ vertical ❏ horizontal ❏ diagonal

   ❏ jagged ❏ other

3. What **lines** are repeated the most?
   _____

4. **Shapes** — check what you see
   ❏ circles ❏ squares ❏ rectangles ❏ triangles

5. What **shapes** are repeated the most?
   _____

6. What kind of **balance** is used?
   symmetrical (each side of the painting is similar) _____
   asymmetrical (each side of the painting is different) _____
   radial (subjects branch out like a wheel from a central point) _____

7. **Focal point** — What is the first thing you see in the painting?
   _____

8. **Purpose** — Check what you think is the artist's primary purpose.
   to imitate nature _____
   to express emotion _____
   to show a creative design _____

9. **Describing words** — check the words below that describe this painting.
   ❏ strength ❏ love ❏ excitement ❏ courage
   ❏ fear ❏ hope ❏ hate ❏ anger
   ❏ loneliness ❏ sadness ❏ peace ❏ death
   ❏ mystery ❏ happiness ❏ othe

10. **Write a paragraph** — Study the painting one more time and your answers to these questions. Then, on a separate sheet of paper, write a paragraph describing this artwork and your reaction to it.

For more information on understanding art works, see the book *Smart Art* by Hollingsworth and Holllingsworth published by Zephyr Press.

Raphael Sanzio
1483-1520

Raphael

Over 500 years ago, one of the greatest artists of the Renaissance period was born. Raphael Sanzio was born on Friday, the 28th day of March 1483. His father served as court painter to the Duke of Urbino, the city in which Raphael was born. He had an older brother and a younger sister, but they both died when they were very young.

Raphael's childhood was one of great sadness. When he was only eight years old, his mother died. His father was soon married again to a woman named Bernardini. Bernardini was not a very good stepmother. Raphael's relatives thought she was bossy and selfish. In 1494 Raphael's father died. Raphael was only 11 years old, and for many years afterward, his uncles, stepmother, and stepsister fought in the courts for control of Raphael and the money and property left to him by his father.

Before he died, Raphael's father taught his young son the basics of painting. After his father's death, Raphael went to study with Perugino, an important painter. Perugino introduced Raphael to the latest ideas in Italian art. He also influenced Raphael's early style of painting.

In 1504 Raphael moved to Florence, then the center of culture in Italy. There he studied the paintings of the great Italian artist, Leonardo da Vinci. Leonardo painted beautiful figures that looked more like ancient Roman gods and goddesses than ordinary people. The balance and beauty of Leonardo's paintings strongly influenced all Renaissance painters, including Raphael.

At the young age of 17, Raphael received his first commission as an artist. Receiving a commission

Paintings by Raphael

means that someone asks an artist to create an artistic work for a fee. Raphael painted an altarpiece for the Baroncio family chapel. It was a large work, almost twelve feet high. Sadly, it was destroyed in an earthquake in 1789.

After painting the altar in 1500, Raphael began to paint less like his teacher Perugino. He studied the anatomy of the human body so that his paintings would be more realistic. He began using new materials such as silverpoint, red chalk, and a wash-effect paint. In addition to studying the paintings of Leonardo, it is likely that he studied Michelangelo as well. However, it was the work of Leonardo that he most cherished and admired. While scholars are not sure, it is possible that the two men knew each other and may have been friends.

ARTISTS

In 1508, Pope Julius II asked Raphael to work for him in Rome. Julius wanted to rebuild Rome to reflect its former glory. Raphael, as well as the best painters, sculptors, and architects in Italy, went to Rome to work. Pope Julius chose Raphael to paint in fresco (the art of painting on wet plaster) the walls of his personal apartment. This was a great honor and further illustrates how highly regarded Raphael's talents were.

It was his work in Rome that led him to produce his masterpiece, *The School Of Athens*. Scholars use this fresco as an example of the best of the classical spirit of the high Renaissance. In the fresco, painted from 1510-11, a group of famous Greek thinkers are gathered around Plato and Aristotle. While Raphael was painting *The School Of Athens*, Michelangelo had nearly completed his famous frescoes on the ceiling of the Sistine Chapel. Raphael's painting seems to have been influenced by Michelangelo, for his placement of the figures is similar to groups in the Sistine Chapel frescoes by Michelangelo.

Raphael's *School of Athens*

Raphael was unable to complete the final room of the Pope's apartment. He died in 1520 after a short illness, He was only 37 years old. He left behind a body of work that to this day is enchanting. Raphael, along with Leonardo and Michelangelo, helped to create the perfect ideals of Renaissance art: beauty, light, and gracefulness.

1. Raphael was born in _____, on _____, 1483.
2. When he was very young, his brother and sister _____
3. When Raphael was eight years old, his mother died and his father married _____.
4. Raphael moved to Florence in 1504 to _____.
5. Two of the artists Raphael studied were _____ and _____.
6. _____ asked Raphael to move to Rome in 1508.
7. Raphael's masterpiece is _____.
8. His masterpiece depicts scholars grouped around _____ and _____.
9. A fresco is a painting painted on _____.
10. Another artist famous for his frescos was _____.
11. His most famous frescos are painted on the ceiling of the _____ _____, and may have influenced _____.
12. Raphael did not finish the work he had begun in Rome because he _____.

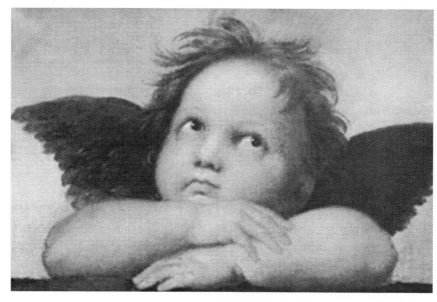

A Raphael Angel

ARTISTS

Connections to the Past

Renaissance Painting of Classical Mythology

A Raphael Angel

The Renaissance began as people started looking back to the art and ideals of the Greeks and Romans. Raphael became renowned as an archeologist. He dug under the streets of Rome and found important monuments and sculptures. Raphael painted a mural he titled *The School of Athens*. This mural included scholars, philosophers, and mathematicians from Greek history. Michelangelo looked toward Greek mythology when he painted the ceiling of the Sistine Chapel. He included The Delphic Sibyl, one of the famous storytellers from Greek mythology. She was the voice of Apollo.

ARTISTS

Imagine that you are an historian living one hundred years in the future. As you study the past and learn about our present, what do you see? Choose a scene that you feel is important for people to know about and draw a picture that tells the story.

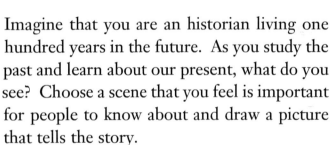

STORIES IN PICTURE

Artists showed information about their time in the paintings they produced. One example of this is Raphael's painting *Saint George and the Dragon*. The horse he painted is rearing back and looking at his rider. During the Renaissance, it was considered part of a prince's training to tame a horse to rear and halt. By including a rearing horse in his painting, Raphael is showing everyone who sees his painting a part of a prince's training. Another painting by Raphael is *An Allegory (Vision of a Knight)*. In this painting, he included symbols that show the choice every young Renaissance knight had to make, the choice between virtue and pleasure.

Raphael's *St. George and the Dragon*

1. Think about the stories in your life and in your city. Draw a picture that tells a story about your life.

2. Draw yourself as St. George.

ARTISTS

43

Leonardo da Vinci
1452-1519

ARTISTS

Leonardo da Vinci

Leonardo da Vinci was a true symbol of the Renaissance. He was the artist who painted *The Last Supper* and the *Mona Lisa*. He was also a sculptor, astronomer, inventor, engineer, and scientist. He performed experiments to discover and confirm hypotheses rather than just accept information from others. He drew over 750 anatomical drawings that were used by medical students. He studied the stars, light, sound, and sight. Among his many accomplishments were the building of a canal, designing a machine for cutting the grooves in screws, improving the water wheel, designing the first machine gun, studying flight, and designing the first parachute. As you can see, Leonardo da Vinci was fascinated by many things, which he explored, designed, built, and drew. He questioned everything because he wanted proof. He was a true Renaissance man!

List 4 things that Leonardo studied:

1.

2.

3.

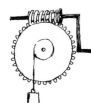

4.

List 4 things that he invented:

1.

2.

3.

4.

Why is Leonardo da Vinci considered a symbol of the Renaissance?

_____

_____

Leonardo

Parachute

Leonardo's Parachute

In 1480 Leonardo da Vinci invented the parachute.

Activity~

Design and make a parachute for a clothespin doll. What materials could you use to make the parachute? How would you attach the parachute? Does the size of the parachute have an effect on the fall? Make a list of materials you might use and draw your experimental designs.

List of Materials Needed: _____
_____

ARTISTS

Ideas of ways to attach clothespin doll to parachute: _____
_____

My Parachute Designs

Leonardo's MONA LISA

Leonardo's *Mona Lisa*

Study the *Mona Lisa*, the world-famous painting by Leonardo da Vinci. Look closely at the expression on her face. Notice how soft and blurry the edges of the body are. Also notice the lighting in the picture. Make a list of many, varied, and unusual words to describe what you see and how it makes you feel.

Activity~

1. Write words to describe *Mona Lisa*. _____
   _____
   _____
   _____

2. Introduce similes with this writing project. Mention the words "as" and "like." For example compare her smile to something else.

Mona Lisa's smile is like <u>a summer day</u>.

Mona Lisa's smile is like _____.

Mona Lisa's smile is like _____.

Her smile is as mysterious as <u>rain</u>.

Her smile is as mysterious as _____.

3. Use these descriptive words to write a poem or paragraph about the painting.
   _____
   _____
   _____
   _____
   _____
   _____

ARTISTS

Albrecht Dürer
1471-1528

Dürer's *Self Portrait*

Albrecht Dürer was a famous German artist. He was very smart. Not only did he write books about art, but he also wrote about science, geometry, government, and human anatomy. In his art books, Dürer tried to explain the difference between ugliness and beauty. He also explained how a person's personality could be shown in a portrait.

Albrecht Dürer was born in Nuremberg, Germany, in 1471. Nuremberg, at the time Dürer was born, was a busy, affluent place. A city of 20,000, it had a stable government and some of the best craftsmen in Europe. Nuremberg crafts, such as armor, guns, silver, bells, toys, locks, cabinets, and musical instruments, were known for their beauty and workmanship.

ARTISTS

Albrecht's father was a goldsmith. Everyone thought that he would apprentice (study under a craftsman) with his father for a while. He learned engraving, which is the art of cutting metal with tools, from his father. This skill would greatly help him later in life.

Albrecht, however, was more interested in the trade of a neighbor, Michael Wolgemut. Wolgemut was a painter, and Dürer at the age of fifteen became an apprentice to him. From Wolgemut he learned to grind and mix paint, prepare wood panels for paintings, and apply gold leaf to the backgrounds of paintings. He did not like being an apprentice, but he learned important skills, such as making woodblock prints. By cutting a design into a block of wood, inking the block, and then pressing it on paper, he could create a print.

Dürer's *Knight Death and Devil*

Woodblock printing was a new process when Dürer was an apprentice, but he quickly mastered it.

Dürer had begun painting before working with Wolgemut. When he was only 13, he began painting self-portraits. A self-portrait is a painting an artist paints of himself. Dürer painted many self-portraits during his life. He must really have wanted to be remembered . . . or maybe he just enjoyed looking at himself.

While studying art as a young man, Dürer became fascinated with Italian art. When he was 23, he visited the city of Venice in Italy. He was there for four years, and when he returned to Germany, he had a new appreciation for art and artists. His trip taught him that artists should not only create things of great beauty, but that they should also study hard, and be gentlemen.

There was a surprise in store for Dürer when he returned home. His parents had arranged for him to marry! Agnes was the wealthy daughter of a master brassworker. While Albrecht and Agnes did not have very much in common, she sold his paintings and managed his business affairs. Indeed, it is doubtful that Dürer would have been as successful without the shrewd (wise) business sense of his wife. Albrecht and Agnes never had any children.

Because Dürer painted so many pictures of himself, kept a diary, and wrote many letters, we know more about him as a person than about any other artist of his time.

Some of Dürer's most famous oil paintings are *Self Portrait* (1500), *The Feast Of The Rose Gardens* (1506), and *Four Apostles* (1526).

Dürer's *Young Hare*

In addition to painting with oil, Dürer was also the first major artist to paint realistic watercolors from nature. He painted landscapes and animals.

The greatest engraver of his time, Dürer used woodcuts to mass produce art that could be sold to common people at fairs and markets. A book he illustrated and published in 1498, *The Apocalypse*, was sold all over Europe and made him famous.

Engraving was more expensive. These prints were sold at higher prices to wealthy clients. Dürer engraved prints illustrating religious subjects and ancient Greek and Roman myths and legends. One of his best known engravings is *Knight, Death, And The Devil* (1513).

ARTISTS

In his later life, Dürer became involved in arguments about religion that were going on in Europe at that time. This religious confusion was known as the Reformation. The Reformation was a time when religious groups broke away from the Catholic church to form Protestant churches.

Dürer showed his concern about these religious disputes in his woodcuts, engravings, and paintings.

Despite his worry about the Reformation, Dürer was able to live his life comfortably. In a time when a poor family of four could live on 15 gulden a year, Albrecht had about 7,000 gulden when he died. Dürer died knowing that his artwork had changed the way people thought about art. He had produced artwork for the poor as well as the rich. A citizen of Nuremberg, he was a scholar, a gentleman, an artist, and a true Renaissance man. He said, "I would rather live a modest life here in Nuremberg where I was born, than achieve fame and riches in other places."

Albrecht Dürer lived to be 57 years old. His oil paintings, watercolors, and prints established him as one of the greatest artists of his time.

Dürer's Chronology

The following events that occurred in Dürer's life are not in order. Number them in the order in which they occurred.

_____   Dürer becomes an apprentice to Michael Wolgemut.

_____   Dürer marries Agnes.

_____   Dürer begins painting self-portraits.

_____   Dürer dies at age 57.

_____   Dürer is born in Nuremberg, Germany, in 1471.

_____   Dürer goes to Venice.

_____   Dürer becomes involved in arguments about the Reformation.

Dürer's Rabbit

Albrecht Dürer was a famous painter and printmaker from Germany. Dürer was the first major artist to paint realistic watercolors from nature. He did many landscapes in the Austrian and Italian Alps.

One of his works from nature, "*Young Hare,*" shows Renaissance interest in observing and recording nature. The Renaissance was the rebirth of attention to classical Greek and Roman art. Dürer used drawing as a way to understand and analyze his world. The watercolor and gouache painting is only about nine inches wide and ten inches tall.

ARTISTS

Activity~

1. Look at Dürer's *Young Hare* and draw one of your own.

2. Now use your five senses as you image you are holding a rabbit. What does the rabbit feel like? What does it smell and see? What does it hear? What does it eat? Where does it live? Now write a descriptive paragraph about the rabbit.

_____

_____

_____

_____

_____

_____

_____

_____

_____

_____

ARTISTS

A Visit To Michelangelo's Studio

Michelangelo's *David*

*Welcome to my studio where I work when I am in Florence. You may remember, I spoke to you earlier. I am Michelangelo and this is my statue of **David**. I have created **David** as a symbol of the Renaissance. All through the Dark Ages, people suffered so greatly that heaven was their only hope.*

Now a new age has dawned. We believe that God wants us to love Him, but that He also wants us to appreciate the beauty and wonder of the earth where He has placed us. We now live in a time, just as the classical Greeks and Romans, when education is important. People in the Renaissance want to learn and to create. We now believe that God wants us to take responsibility for what happens to us.

I want David to represent the recently found confidence of human beings. I want him to be a shaper of his own destiny. Large, ugly forces will not make him cower. He faces those dangers directly. David eyed Goliath and knew he could win if he used his faith and the intelligence that God gave him.

Excuse me now; I must work. The Pope wants me to return to Rome to paint on that wretched ceiling of his, the Sistine Chapel. I really do not like painting. However, I do like architecture. I have a great idea for creating a dome for St. Peter's Cathedral in Rome. If you look at Brunelleschi's dome here in Florence, you will get an idea of what I hope to do.

Brunelleschi's Dome in Florence

Thanks for coming to the studio. I had better get back to the work God has given me to do while I still have time.

ARTISTS

53

MICHELANGELO QUESTIONS

1. Why do you think that Michelangelo chose to sculpt *David*? _____
   _____
   _____
   _____

ARTISTS

2. Why do you think that Michelangelo does not want to work on the Sistine Chapel? _____
   _____
   _____
   _____

3. How does Michelangelo think that the Renaissance is different from the Middle Ages? _____
   _____
   _____

4. What architect does Michelangelo like? _____
   _____

5. Who would you paint or sculpt to represent our time period? _____
   _____

Explain why you selected this person: _____
_____
_____
_____
_____

Michelangelo

Michelangelo

One of the most famous artists who ever lived was a man named Michelangelo. He was a sculptor, painter, and architect. He lived and worked near Florence, Italy, during the Renaissance.

Michelangelo was lucky to grow up in Florence. This city was the artistic center of Europe during the Renaissance. When he was 13, he joined a workshop where he learned the skills of art. It was like a university of art. By the time he was 15, the masters were paying him instead of charging him for his lessons.

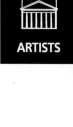
ARTISTS

Michelangelo wanted to learn sculpture. By the time he was 17, he was sculpting for Lorenzo de' Medici, the great prince of Florence. Michelangelo worked on sculpting the rest of his life. He created figures similar to those created in ancient Greece and Rome. His statues bulge with muscles. Their flesh looks real enough to feel warm to the touch even though the statues are made of cold marble.

Next Michelangelo went to work for the church in Rome. Here he was commissioned to create religious sculptures and paintings. The Pope of the Roman Catholic Church used Michelangelo as an architect also. Michelangelo designed tombs for the pope and a dome for Saint Peter's church.

Michelangelo lived to be almost 90 years old. He died working on a statue.

Florence, Italy

MICHELANGELO The Sculptor

Michelangelo created numerous pieces of art, but his most famous sculpture is probably *David*. The statue *David* is nearly 14 feet high and free-standing. It shows David with his slingshot about to kill the evil giant Goliath.

Pretend that you are Michelangelo and that you have been commissioned to create the statue of *David*.

David

ARTISTS

What would you do to plan your statue?

_____
_____
_____

What materials and equipment might you need?

_____
_____
_____

What steps are you going to take to create your statue?

_____
_____
_____

What are some problems you might encounter?

_____
_____
_____

Predict what the outcome will be.

_____
_____
_____

MICHELANGELO The Painter

Michelangelo also created numerous paintings even though he did not consider himself a painter. His most famous painting is the ceiling of the Sistine Chapel in the Vatican in Rome. The ceiling is over 60 feet high, the height of a three-story building. The subject, the history of the creation of the world, is done with almost 300 figures. It measures 132 feet by 64 feet, more than the size of two tennis courts. It took Michelangelo 1,600 days, or 4 years and 5 months, to paint it. He did it lying on his back.

Imagine that you have been commissioned to paint this ceiling.

Sistine Chapel, Vatican, Rome

ARTISTS

How would you begin planning this project?
_____
_____

What materials and equipment might you need?
_____
_____

What steps would you take to create your painting?
_____
_____

What are some problems you might encounter?
_____
_____

Predict what the outcome will be. _____
_____
_____

MICHELANGELO The Architect

Not only did Michelangelo create famous sculptures and paintings; he was an architect as well. He designed some tombs for a pope, but his most famous work of architecture is probably the dome of St. Peter's Cathedral. It can be seen from many places throughout Rome. It is part of the Roman skyline.

St. Peter's Cathedral in Rome

ARTISTS

Pretend that you are Michelangelo and that you have been commissioned to create the dome for the top of St. Peter's Cathedral.

How would you plan your dome?
___
___
___

What materials and equipment might you need?
___
___
___

What steps would you take to create your dome?
___
___
___

What are some problems you might encounter?
___
___
___

Predict what the outcome will be.
___
___
___

Sistine Chapel, Vatican Rome

MICHAELANGELO'S ASSISTANT

Michelangelo often took on large projects — the ceiling of the Sistine Chapel, the statue of *David*, the dome of St. Peter's Cathedral. He preferred to do everything himself, but it was not always possible. When he had assistants, he wanted everything done exactly as he wished. He was a brilliant artist but a difficult and temperamental man who might become furious at an assistant's mistake and fire the person.

If you had lived at that time, would you work for Michelangelo? Would the chance to learn from a master artist be worth the conditions?

ARTISTS

Activity~

List the many, varied, and unusual pros and cons of working for Michaelangelo.

PROS	*CONS*

____ I would work for Michelangelo.
____ I would not work for Michelangelo.

My reasons for this decision are:

_____
_____
_____

RENAISSANCE ARCHITECTS

1400s Architecture

Brunelleschi's Dome

Ghiberti's Doors

During the Renaissance, architects created buildings with features like those of classical Greek and Roman buildings. They wanted people to be reminded of classical ideals when they looked at Renaissance buildings. Buildings began to be symmetrical, solid, balanced, and stable.

Filippo Brunelleschi was one of the most famous Renaissance architects. However, his fame had not come easily. In 1403, when he lost the Baptistry Door's competition to Lorenzo Ghiberti, Brunelleschi was embarrassed and angry. To regain his dignity, he went to Rome, where he studied classical Roman architecture, making careful measurement of classical buildings. He used his setback as a time to learn things about architecture that no one else in the Renaissance knew at that time.

Brunelleschi's knowledge helped him win the next competition that he entered. The competition was to build a dome for the Florence Cathedral. In Rome, Brunelleschi had studied and measured the Pantheon as well as other ancient buildings. Instead of one oculus at the top of the dome as in the Pantheon, Brunelleschi proposed eight oculi looking out at the city of Florence in different directions.

The dome brought lasting fame to Brunelleschi. His dome was the largest built since the Pantheon and the tallest ever at that time.

Brunelleschi's Dome

The dome is composed of an inner and outer shell with both shells anchored to the eight large ribs. Brunelleschi invented a hoisting machine that the builders used to lift the heavy materials to the work areas. His dome, built between 1420 and 1436, was an engineering masterpiece.

Activity~

Create a design for a set of double doors. Put the doors on the front of a building with a dome that includes classical Greek and Roman features such as rounded arches, pediments, and columns. Look at the Timeline on page 6 for examples of these features.

ARCHITECTS

1500s Architecture

Palladio

Palladio's real name was Andrea di Pietro (1508-1580). His first patron began calling him Palladio after the goddess of wisdom, Pallas. Palladio and his pupils turned Vicenza into one of the most beautiful cities in Italy by the numerous buildings that they designed and built there.

ARCHITECTS

One of Palladio's most famous buildings is Villa Rotunda. It is an example of how Renaissance architects applied what they knew about classical Greek and Roman architecture it to their own designs.

Thomas Jefferson, a founding father of the United States, owned a copy of an architecture book by Palladio. Jefferson used the book to guide his building of Monticello and other classically styled buildings in the New World.

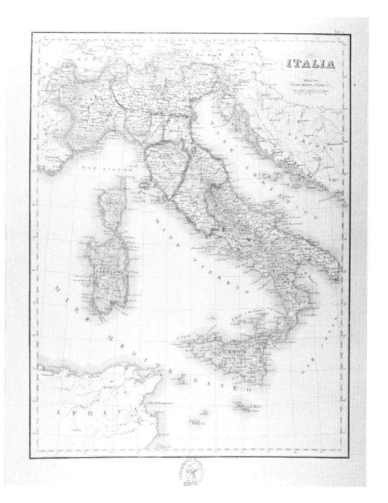

Ancient Map of Italy

Today we still see Palladio's influence. The semicircular windows that are used in homes and public buildings today are called Palladian windows.

Michelangelo

Michelangelo was an architect as well as an artist and sculptor. He designed the dome for St. Peter's Cathedral based on the work of Brunelleschi.

Michelangelo's Dome

Activity~

1. Design a home using classical features of dome, rounded arches, pediments, and columns. Include both Brunelleschi's round oculi windows and Palladian semicircular windows.

ARCHITECTS

2. What do you think is the purpose of a dome? What does it do for a building? Would you want one on your home?

_____
_____
_____
_____

63

Renaissance Writers/Music

Renaissance Music

Renaissance Musician

During the Middle Ages, the church held the keys to education. With the invention of the printing press, knowledge became available to more people. No longer did the church have exclusive access to information. During the Renaissance, a good education became a status symbol to middle and upper class families and always included training in music. Music began to play a bigger part in the lives of more people. This brought about many changes to both sacred and secular music.

In the Middle Ages, sacred music, the religious music of the church, had its own style in the traditional Roman Catholic church. This plain chant style, a singular voice line performed by a professional group of monks in the Latin language, is often referred to as Gregorian chant. By the time of the Renaissance, a new polyphonic style had emerged. Polyphony consists of two or three individual melody lines moving simultaneously. The polyphonic style was used in the sacred music form called the motet. The text or words of the motet were in Latin and of a religious nature.

Sacred Music

The mass was another important sacred music form. The mass is the worship service for the Roman Catholic church. However, music written for this service is also called a mass. The mass consisted of five different parts: the Kyrie, Gloria, Credo, Sanctus, and Angus dei.

By the time of the Renaissance, most

people did not speak Latin. But when they attended Roman Catholic church services, the music and service were in Latin, a language they did not even understand. Martin Luther and the Protestant Reformation came along during the Renaissance and made a change. The new Protestant church emerged, led by Martin Luther and his followers. The church service was changed to the language of the common people, and the music was sung by the whole congregation in their native tongue in the form of hymns.

Secular music, music of the people similar to our 'pop' music, also changed in the Renaissance. In the Middle Ages, most secular music was written for singing voices and performed by professional musicians known as minstrels, jongleurs, troubadours, trouveres, or minnesingers. All of these names refer to musicians in various parts of Europe who traveled, singing songs about love or political satire. Often these performances included juggling or acrobatics.

Secular music in the Renaissance came in three types: chansons, dance music, and madrigals. The chanson was usually written for three voices. Either of the lower two voices could be played on an instrument. Dance music was like the chanson except none of the melody lines were sung. These melody lines were played on instruments and had names such as pavane, saltarello, allemande, galliard, or ronde. The madrigal was similar to the sacred motet with its four to six melody lines but contained secular lyrics.

Since music in the Middle Ages was written for the singing voice, the Renaissance idea of writing music for instruments was new. Renaissance composers wrote music for instruments but not for specific instruments as is the custom now. They simply wrote a melody line, and whatever instruments were available in the community (within the appropriate range) played the part. Some of the Renaissance instruments were the crumhorn, recorder, lute, viol, shawm, and sackbutt. Percussion lines were rarely written, but often improvised during the performance.

WRITERS/ MUSIC

Activity~

1) Polyphony is two or more voices singing individual melodies. Find a partner. Try singing "London Bridge" and "Mary Had a Little Lamb" simultaneously. That's polyphony! (Other songs to try: "Swing Low, Sweet Chariot" and "All Night, All Day.")

2) Look in a Protestant hymnal for hymns written by Martin Luther. ("A Mighty Fortress is our God" is one of the most famous.) Look for hymns that were written between 1400 and 1600. Make a list of these hymns. Try to play them or find someone who can to hear what Renaissance hymns sound like.

Lute Player

3) Shawm, crumhorn, lute . . . what unusual names for instruments! Use your imagination and make a quick sketch to predict what these instruments might look like. Now use an encyclopedia or other reference book to see what these instruments truly look like. Compare your pictures to the real thing. Make a poster of the Renaissance instruments. Try to make a model of one of the Renaissance instruments.

4) Find a CD of Renaissance music at a library or music store. Try to find a recording using original instruments. Make a chart comparing this music to your favorite music.

5) Compare and contrast music in the Middle Ages and music in the Renaissance. Make a chart of your information.

6) Write a paragraph about how the music of the Renaissance reflects the trends of the Renaissance.

_____
_____
_____
_____
_____

Ben Jonson
1572-1637

Ben Jonson

Ben Jonson is a famous Renaissance writer. A playwright, poet, actor and teacher, Jonson's life was at times difficult. Born in England in 1572, Jonson's father died not long afterward He was adopted by his stepfather who educated him in the trade of bricklaying. After serving in the army in Flanders, Jonson returned to London and began work as an actor and playwright.

Success and conflict quickly caught up with Ben Jonson. His first play, *Every Man In His Humour*, was performed in 1598, with a leading role played by William Shakespeare. It was a great success, and Jonson was established as a fine playwright. However, later that year, Jonson was jailed briefly for killing a fellow actor in a duel. He was spared execution by claiming "benefit of clergy," which meant that, because he could read and write, he should be treated as a special case. He later went to jail again for making fun of the Scottish government. England's king was from Scotland, and he did not take kindly to Jonson's sense of humor!

WRITERS/MUSIC

After his bouts with the jailer, Jonson spent the next four years writing plays to satirize or make fun of other writers. Jonson and these writers, Thomas Dekker and John Marston, eventually settled their differences and in fact wrote some plays together. In addition to Dekker and Marston, Jonson's friends included William Shakespeare, John Donne, and Francis Bacon. They believed

Renaissance Drama

that writing was important, greatly influenced the artists of their time, and still are influential today.

As Ben Jonson became older, he became wiser and gentler. His plays became very popular at court and were performed often. His poetry was popular as well — he was proclaimed England's poet laureate in 1616. Jonson's poetry expressed his feelings about everything: from funny poems written about his friends, wicked poems composed to humiliate his enemies, and sad, poignant poems written about the deaths of his children. Jonson wrote about everything that was important to him.

Ben Jonson became the first English writer to have all of his works published together in one book, *The Works Of Benjamin Jonson.* It was considered vain that time to publish one's own work, although many writers were quick to follow his lead.

Ben Jonson died in 1637.

What helped Jonson become a wiser person? _____
_____
_____
_____
_____
_____
_____
_____
_____

Ben Jonson

CROSSWORD

Across

3. Jonson's first occupation learned from stepfather
4. Using writing to make fun of something
5. Official poet of a state or nation (two words)
6. Special rights given to people who could read and write (3 words)
7. First play written by Jonson, *Every Man In His* _____

Down

1. One of Jonson's enemies who later became his friend
2. Where Jonson served in the army
4. Famous playwright in Jonson's time who played the lead in his first play

answers: poet laureate, benefit of clergy, Flanders, Dekker, satirize, Shakespeare, Humour, bricklayer

Twelfth Night

Shakespeare's comedic play *Twelfth Night* is set in a land called Illyria. The play begins with the girl Viola landing in a strange country after surviving a shipwreck in which she believes her brother Sebastian has drowned. Viola disguises herself as a boy and becomes a member of the court of Duke Orsino, the ruler of Illyria.

William Shakespeare

Duke Orsino is in love with Lady Olivia. Unfortunately Lady Olivia is in mourning after the death of her brother and has forsaken love. Viola, acting as the page of Duke Orsino, is dispatched to Lady Olivia's home in order to impress her about the character of Duke Orsino. All of these wonderful plans become undone when we discover that Viola has fallen in love with the Duke, and Lady Olivia (believing Viola to be a man) has fallen in love with Viola!

Characters from *Twelfth Night*

To further confuse matters, Lady Olivia has a butler Malvolio. Malvolio is also in love with Lady Olivia, much to the amusement of the other characters that live at court with Lady Olivia: Sir Toby Belch, Fabian, Sir Andrew, and Maria the maid. They dislike Malvolio, and in this scene from *Twelfth Night*, they plan to play a trick on Malvolio.

(In walk Sir Toby, Fabian, and Sir Andrew.)

Toby *Come this way, Signior Fabian.*

Fabian *Yes, I'll come. If I were to miss a minute of this sport, I would die of sadness.*

Toby   *Will you really be glad to have that rascal come by some notable shame?*

Fabian   *I would exult in it sir. You know he was responsible for ruining my favor with the Lady Olivia.*

Toby   *Then don't worry, for we will shame him black and blue, shall we not, Sir Andrew?*

Andrew   *If we don't it shall be the pity of our lives.*

Toby   *Here comes the little villain now.*

(Enter Maria. She is carrying a letter.)

Toby   *No wait, 'tis my fine lass instead!*

Maria with the letter

Maria   *Get ye all behind that shrub! Malvolio's coming down this walk! He has been out there in the garden practicing behavior to his own shadow for more than a half-hour. Watch him, for I know this letter will make a total fool of him. Hide, in the name of our jest, for here comes the trout that must be caught with the bait.*

(Maria places the letter on the ground. Sir Toby, Fabian, Sir Andrew, and Maria hide behind a bush. Enter Malvolio.)

Malvolio   *Tis but luck, all is luck. Maria once told me that Olivia did like me. Besides, Lady Olivia treats me with more respect than anyone else that follows here. I wonder.*

Toby   *Oh, listen to him go on!*

Fabian   *Oh peace! How highly he regards himself, and foolish it makes him appear!*

Andrew   *Quiet! I can't hear!*

Toby   *Peace, I say!*

Malvolio   *To be Count Malvolio!*

Toby   *What a villain.*

Andrew   *We should kill him, kill him I say!*

Toby   *Peace, peace.*

Malvolio   *Other ladies of nobility have married beneath their stations. Look at Lady Strachy. She married her dresser!*

Andrew   *Let me at him!*

Fabian   *Ssssh! Listen to how deeply he is into this fantasy!*

Malvolio   *Let's see, after we are married about three months, I'll call all my officers to me. I'll come in my velvet dressing gown and remind them all of their places and of mine as well.*

Toby   *Fire and brimstone!*

Malvolio   *I'll remind Sir Toby of his indebtedness to me and pray beseech him to reform his drunken and slovenly ways.*

Toby   *I'll kill him!*

Fabian   *Peace, peace. Do you want him to hear us?*

(Malvolio walks along the path and spies the letter that Maria placed there.)

Malvolio   *What's this? (Reads) "To my beloved." Why, this is Lady Olivia's writing indeed. "No man must know, but I must let you know that I am in love with you. Oh, that I had not committed myself to that wretched promise! Please remember, that although we cannot now be together, that surely someday, perhaps in heaven, we will be as one. Keep thyself pure for me, and remember who complimented you so on being cross-gartered in yellow stockings. Farewell, and remember that I love you." I can't quite make out who this missive is addressed to. I see M, A, L, why, that's me, Malvolio! She wrote this letter to me!*

(The group behind the bush breaks into a big show of silent laughter as Malvolio dances and kisses the letter.)

Malvolio　*I'm going directly to my room. If Lady Olivia likes my yellow stockings so well, why, I'll go and put them right on.*

Malvolio reading the letter

(Malvolio leaves and the others come from behind the bush.)

Fabian　*I would not give a thousand dollars to have missed that.*

Andrew　*Nor I.*

Toby　*I ask for nothing more from life except perhaps another jest like that.*

Maria　*I believe that is as funny as ever as I have seen, but how will we know if our jest was truly a success?*

Fabian　*Believe me, if you see Malvolio approach our Lady Olivia. He'll be wearing cross-gartered stockings of a most odious hue, and he'll have a smile as big as his ugly face. Lady Olivia will be so sickened to see it, he will be most in her disfavor.*

Toby　*Let us go then, to see the fruits of our labor!*

(Everyone exits.)

Incognito Titles — Plays by William Shakespeare

Below are the titles of several of Shakespeare's play in disguise. Use a dictionary or thesaurus to help you decode the titles, or use the plays in the word box below to help you.

One Portion of a Dozen Blackness
_____

The Domestication of the Virago
_____

A Great Amount of Hubbub Concerning Naught
_____

A Median Season 12-Hour Period of Darkness Illusion
_____

A Specific Tumult
_____

The Peddler of an Italian City Built On a Series of Canals
_____

Everythings Satisfactory that Concludes Satisfactorily
_____

WRITERS/ MUSIC

Word Box (not all of the titles below will be used; none will be used twice)

Renaissance
WORD BOX

The Merry Wives of Windsor	The Comedy of Errors	The Two Noble Kinsmen
	All's Well that Ends Well	The Tempest
Twelfth Night	The Taming of the Shrew	The Winter's Tale
The Merchant of Venice	A Midsummer Night's Dream	
Much Ado About Nothing		

Now that you have done such great detective work, try some of your own. Use the titles in the word box on page 74 to make up your own incognito titles.

Shakespeare Matching

Language during Shakespeare's time was rich, descriptive, and flowing. Try to match the sayings from Shakespeare's time to their meanings today.

_____ Sad, all alone, not long I musing sat . . .
        Fletch, 1593

_____ When forty winters shall besiege thy brow . . .
        Shakespeare, 1600

_____ Alas, my love, ye do me wrong to cast me off.
        Anonymous

_____ Silence augmented grief; writing increaseth rage.
        Lord Brook, 1593

_____ On a hill that graced the plain/ Thyrsis sate, a comely swain.
        William Browne, 1600

_____ Thou dolt, why does chat of this? Thyself a rustic born . . .
        George Turberville, 1567

_____ Both robbed of air, we both lie in one ground/Both whom one fire had burned, one water drowned.
        John Donne, 1633

_____ Time will not be ours forever./He at length our good will sever.
        Ben Jonson, 1616

_____ Mistrust me not till all be known . . .
        Sir Thomas Wyatt, 1536

_____ Tell me where is fancy bred, or in the heart or in the fead?
        Shakespeare, 1596

A. Thyrsis, a good-looking guy, sat on a hill.

B. Trust me until you know the full story.

C. When you are forty years old . . .

D. We will not live forever, eventually we will die.

E. Being quiet makes you feel sad, putting your thoughts to paper makes you more angry.

F. I sat by myself thinking for a while.

G. We had very different deaths, yet here we lie in the same ground.

H. You idiot! Why are you talking when we all know you are a backwards country person?

I. I love you and you are mean to ignore me so rudely.

J. Does love begin in your head or in your heart?

WRITERS/ MUSIC

76

RENAISSANCE
SCIENCE & MATH

Arch and Lintel Experiments

The Greeks were pure scientists. They observed, calculated, and recorded their observations and discoveries. They built beautiful buildings, often using columns and beams. The Romans took the information they learned from the Greeks, refined it, and applied it to everyday life and everyday problems. The Romans moved from column/beam construction used by the Greeks to column/arch construction. The Renaissance builders renewed these concepts and used arches in many ways.

Greek Parthenon

Roman Pantheon

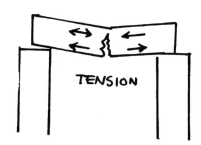
Post and Lintel Construction

Keystone Arch

Roman Aqueduct

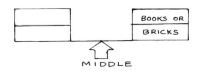

Experiment to see if an arch is stronger than a beam.

Materials
Poster board, 12 inches long and 4 inches wide
4 similar heavy books or 4 bricks
weight: pennies, metal washers
ruler and a pencil

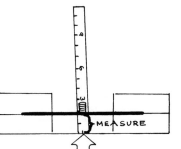

Experiment I: Beam/Lintel
Place 2 bricks (or books) 6 inches apart.
Mark the midpoint between the 2 bricks with a piece of tape.
Mark the poster board at the middle.
Place the poster board on the 2 bricks, so the line in the middle of the poster board is above the midpoint line of tape.

SCIENCE & MATH

77

Place 2 bricks on top of the first 2 (to hold the poster board in place).

Measure the distance from the tape to the poster board _____
Put on one weight (penny or washer) and measure again _____
Put a second weight on the first and measure again _____
Put a third weight on the second and measure again _____
✭ Continue adding weight until the beam collapses. How much concentrated weight did your beam hold? __4 washers__

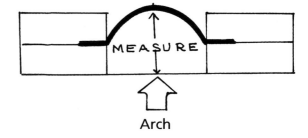

Arch

Experiment II: Arch
Now take your beam and mark 2 inches from each end. Fold both ends up. Place the folded ends of the beam between the 4 bricks so your poster board now forms an arch. Be sure the line in the middle of your poster board arch lines up with the midpoint line of the tape.

Measure the height of the arch from the tape to the poster board _____
Put one weight on the center of the arch and measure again _____
Put a second weight on the first and measure again _____
Put a third weight on the second and measure again _____
Continue adding weight if you can.
✭ How many weights did you put on the arch before it collapsed? __39 washers__
✭ Which shape (beam or arch) held the most weight? __The arch__
Do you know why? _____
If you were building a bridge using columns and arches to support the bridge (beam), what would happen if the columns were very close together? _____
_____
Could the water flow smoothly down the river past the columns? _____
_____
Could water erode the columns? _____
_____
Draw a better design for a bridge here: _____
_____

SCIENCE & MATH

78

Renaissance Dome

Using arches, Romans built bridges (that are still in use today) and aqueducts to carry water as far as 15 miles. The Renaissance builders also used arches to construct beautiful domed buildings. In buildings, the barrel vault of a dome creates more height and beauty.

Roman Aqueduct

Renaissance Dome

Try this:
Materials
Poster board, stapler or tape, markers or crayons

Procedure
Cut the poster board into:

1 strip 18 inches long and 4 inches wide
3 strips 12 inches long and 1 inch wide
Mark 1 inch from both ends of all the strips.
Decorate the strips.
Bring the 2 ends of the 4 inch poster board together to make a cylinder. Tape or staple. This is now a base.
Attach one end of a 1 inch poster board onto the top of the base, and attach the other end directly across. Each end should overlap the base inch (at the mark).
Repeat the above step twice, criss-crossing the strips. You have created a beautiful domed.

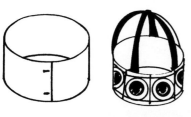

How tall would your dome be without the drum or barrel?

_____

How tall is your dome with the drum?

_____

Extension
What do you build if you place several arches each in front of the others?

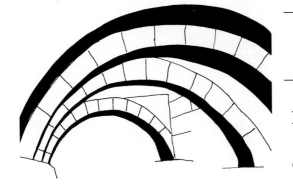
Roman Arches

SCIENCE & MATH

79

Make Concrete

Mount Vesuvius Italy

The other component of long-lasting buildings was concrete, invented by the Egyptians, used by the Greeks, improved by the Romans, and used again by Renaissance builders. Concrete is a mixture of cement (which is powdered limestone and clay), water, sand, and gravel. Near Mount Vesuvius, a volcano that erupted in 79 AD, the Romans found volcanic ash, added it to their limestone mixture, and ended up with a very strong concrete that could harden even under water. The Romans used this super strong concrete for bridges and aqueducts. The Renaissance builders also used it for arches, especially to form the domes on their buildings.

Experiment I

Safety glasses and rubber gloves must be worn during this experiment!

Materials

    Cement (not "redi-mix"). You can buy this at a building supply store.
    Sand, gravel, water, kitty litter
    Thread (nylon works best), about 10 feet
    9 ounce plastic cups (punch two holes near the rim of each cup, directly across from each other)
    A large, flat bowl so this experiment will not be messy.
    Cardboard (tape the cardboard together to make a box 4 inches long, 1 inch wide, and 1 inch tall.) You will need 5 of these boxes for molds.
    Scissors and tape (to make the boxes)
    Two supports (Pringles cans, 3# coffee cans, or stacks of books)

CARDBOARD BOX MOLD (MAKE 5)

SCIENCE & MATH

Procedure

Brick 1:   Make the cement mixture according to the directions on the sack, using the sand, gravel, and water. Pour inch deep in one mold.

Brick 2:   Make a second mixture using only water and the mix and gravel (no sand). Pour this inch deep in another mold.

Brick 3: Make the next block using only water, the mix, and sand (no gravel).
Brick 4: Make the next block using only water, the mix, and kitty litter.
Brick 5: Make the last block using only water and the mix (no sand, gravel or kitty litter).

After the blocks are dry, remove them from the molds. Remember which mixture made each block!

Place each end of the first block on a support.

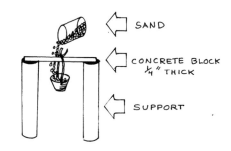

Tie one end of an 18-inch thread through one hole in a cup, loop it over the concrete block, and tie the other end through the other hole in the cup so the cup hangs below the block.

Slowly pour sand into the cup until the block breaks.

Measure the sand you used in a measuring cup, or weigh it if you have a small kitchen scale. How much sand did you use?

Repeat this procedure for each block:
  Amount of sand for second block? _____
  Amount of sand for third block? _____
  Amount of sand for fourth block? _____
  Amount of sand for fifth block? _____

Which concrete block was the strongest? The weakest?

Experiment II

Do this same experiment with bricks made from modeling clay.
  Brick 1: plain clay
  Brick 2: clay with sand (just a small amount)
  Brick 3: clay with grass
  Brick 4: clay with spaghetti
  Brick 5: clay with a mixture of sand, grass, and spaghetti

After the clay bricks harden, do the same experiments you did with the concrete blocks. Which brick was the strongest? Why?

Experiment with Printing

In 1450, Gutenberg invented the European printing press, making written knowledge available to a large population. The use of metal plates for printing diminished the formidable task of copying everything by hand.

Gutenberg

In 1465 the first printed music was produced. Printing was faster than copying by hand but still it was a slow process. By 1501 about 35,000 books with 10 million copies had been produced, and in 1566 newspapers were beginning. Black lead pencils were first used in 1500. It was 1565 before pencils were first manufactured in England. It is interesting that pencils were not available until several decades after printing was invented.

What was used instead? _____

_____

What is used now? _____

Potato carved for printing

Activity
Make a block print using an apple or potato.

Materials
Knife, apple or potato, ink pad or paint, and paper

Procedure
Decide on a design for your print. Cut off the end of the potato or apple so the surface is flat. Draw your design on the flat surface using a pencil, which will make a small groove in the surface. Scrape away the surface that will not be a part of the design. Paint your raised design or press the design into the inkpad. Now press the design on a piece of paper.

What do you think we will use in the future? _____

_____

MAGNIFYING THE WORLD

The Renaissance scientists were eager to learn more about nature. They used telescopes to study objects that were far away and microscopes to enlarge the images of small objects.

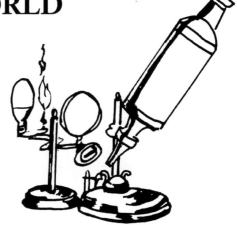

Early Renaissance Microscope

Activity~

Using a magnifying glass or microscope, carefully observe and record life around you. Be sure to label everything you examine. Some suggestions are: hair, hand, shirt, pencil shavings, paper, grass, ants, sand, sugar, and the Sunday comics. Use the space below to write about your observations and draw pictures of your most interesting findings.

_____
_____
_____
_____

SCIENCE & MATH

Renaissance Invention

Lead Pencils Do Not Contain Lead!

Renaissance Writer

During the ancient Greek and Roman times, people used flat cakes of lead which made light marks on papyrus (a type of paper). This worked, but needed improvement. In the 1500s, which was the last part of the Renaissance, graphite was found to mark better on paper. This idea was later improved in the 1700s when sticks of a graphite mixture made of graphite and clay were placed inside cases of wood. What does that sound like? Why, our modern pencil, of course!

So why do we call these pencils "lead pencils" and the graphite inside a "piece of lead?" It's a throwback to Greek and Roman years when lead was really used. When our modern version of pencils were first made, people thought the graphite mixture must contain lead. They were wrong, but the name stuck!

Activity~

Imagine yourself as a Renaissance person with your first pencil. Make a list of nouns that could describe the future of you and the pencil. Then make a list of strong, action verbs of what you and your pencil could do together.

Nouns_____

_____

Strong, action verbs_____

_____

On a separate sheet of paper, write a poem about what you and the pencil might do. It does not have to rhyme.

OBSERVING THE NATURAL WORLD

What Does Your Hand Look Like?

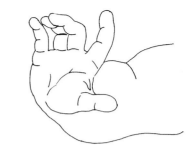

Part I

Renaissance Woman

Hold your hand out in front of you and look at it closely. This is how people basically observed objects in the world before the Renaissance—with the naked eye. Describe your hand in the spaces below.

Adjectives
shape _____
color _____
texture _____
other features _____

Nouns
  What is my hand? _____

Verbs
  What can my hand do? _____

Similes
Use your imagination
  My hand is like a _____

Draw your hand here:

SCIENCE & MATH

Part II

The Renaissance was a time of inventions and discoveries, including the microscope. The concept of the microscope was discovered accidentally by the Dutch eyeglass maker Hans Janssen in 1590.

Early Microscope

A microscope which enlarges an image many times larger than its size This invention is one of the most important tools of science. With the microscope researchers can see a world too small to be seen by the naked eye.

Study your hand again with a magnifying glass. If you are surprised by how differently your hand looks when it is magnified, so were the people of the Renaissance. The microscope helped them discover a whole new world — a micro-world. Describe the "new" hand that you see in the spaces below.

Hans Janssen

Adjectives
  shape _____

  color _____

  texture _____

  other features _____

Nouns
  What is my hand? _____

Verbs
  What can my hand do? _____

Similes
Use your imagination
  My hand is like a _____

Draw part of your magnified hand here:

PART III

Haiku is a Japanese poetic structure with three lines and definite syllable counts for each line. Haiku is normally written to describe nature, but this purpose will be changed slightly for the poem below.

Look at the words and drawings of your hand with and without a microscope. Think about how differently people saw the world before and after the Renaissance.

Using these ideas, write a three-line unrhymed poem in the spaces below. The required syllables for each line are marked in parentheses.

My Hand

_____(5)

_____(7)

_____(5)

Renaissance of Numbers

As you know, the word Renaissance means rebirth. This was especially true in the scientific area of mathematics. Scientists were very interested in studying the meaning of old Arab and Greek teachings. Many new and challenging mathematical ideas developed from these studies. With the recent invention of the printing press, it was possible for scientists to share their ideas with others around the world.

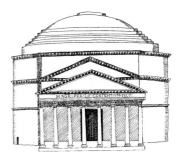
Roman Pantheon

Until the Renaissance period, most scientists were still working with the Roman system of numbers. They soon realized that solving more challenging math problems was difficult using this system. A different number system had just been developed during the Medieval time period. It was known as the Hindu-Arabic system. Renaissance mathematicians adopted this system and improved it so that it was much easier to read and understand. They called this improved system the Arabic number system or the modern system. It is the same one we use today. Scientists found that by using this system, it was much easier to explain their new ideas in mathematics to others.

Here are some examples of numbers written in both Roman numerals and Arabic (modern) systems.

Roman numeral	Arabic (modern)
VIII	8
XXXIII	33
CCLXXIII	273
MVCCCXLVII	4,347

Which system do you think would be easier to use? _____
Why? _The Arabic (modern) system would be easier to use because it is easy to see the number and not have to add up the numbers._

89

You are a great mathematician living during the Renaissance period, and you are asked to create a new number system that would be easier to work with than the current one. Can you create a better system?

Below are numbers 1 through 20 plus some other important numbers in both the Roman and Arabic (modern) number system. Next to them is a space for you to create your own system.

Renaissance Man

Number word	Roman Numeral	Arabic (modern) Number System	Your Number System
one	I	1	
two	II	2	
three	III	3	
four	IV	4	
five	V	5	
six	VI	6	
seven	VII	7	
eight	VIII	8	
nine	IX	9	
ten	X	10	
eleven	XI	11	
twelve	XII	12	
thirteen	XIII	13	
fourteen	XIV	14	
fifteen	XV	15	
sixteen	XVI	16	
seventeen	XVII	17	
eighteen	XVIII	18	
nineteen	XIX	19	
twenty	XX	20	
fifty	L	50	
one hundred	C	100	
five hundred	D	500	
one thousand	M	1,000	

What is the name your number system? __Emoji System__

What symbols did you use to create your numbers? __Different creative emoji's__

Why did you choose these symbols for your numbers? __They are easy to write and fun + creative.__

How is your number system easier to use? __It is easy because they are simple drawings that represent different numbers.__

MATH SIGNS

Another improvement during the Renaissance that helped make understanding mathematics easier was the invention of the plus (+), minus (-), and equal (=) signs that we use today. These symbols made it much easier to understand what was supposed to be done with a given set of numbers.

For example:
>Would you know what to do if you were given the following set of numbers?   (14, 6, 8)
>
>You might be able to think of many different ways to use these numbers together, but how would you know which way to choose?
>
>Now look at the same set of numbers again. Only this time we will use mathematical symbols: (14 - 6 = 8)
>
>You can tell right away what you are supposed to do with this set of numbers to find the answer.

Renaissance Thinkers

Below are some incomplete math problems. The (+) and (-) signs are missing. Look at the equal sign in each problem to help you decide which one of the signs you need to put in the blank in order to complete the problem correctly.

1. 6 __ 10 = 16

2. 22 __ 12 = 10

3. 24 __ 16 = 8

4. 75 __ 25 = 100

5. 20 __ 15 = 5

6. 500 __ 55 = 555

7. 29 __ 7 = 36

8. 50 __ 25 = 25

9. 1000 __ 100 = 1100

10. 8 __ 8 = 16

Now create some of your own.

SCIENCE & MATH

answers:
1. +, 2. -, 3. -, 4. +, 5. -, 6. +, 7. +, 8. -, 9. +, 10. +.

Mathematics

Crossword

Across

3. Time period before the Renaissance.
5. Number system used until Medieval times.
8. Number system introduced during the Medieval times.
10. Time period known for new beginnings.
12. Written name for the number 2.
13. Name for the (+) sign.
15. The _____ press made it easy for scientists to share new ideas with each other.
16. Written name for the number 11.
17. Written name for the number 20.

94

Down
1. During the Renaissance new interest developed in _____ area of science.
2. Operation used to solve 25-10 = 15.
4. Operation used to solve 10+6 = 16.
6. Operation used to solve 25-10 = 15.
7. During the Renaissance, scientists were interested in studying the meaning of Arabic and _____ teachings.
9. Written name for the number 50.
10. Renaissance means _____.
11. Name for the (=) sign.
14. Number system in use today, created by perfecting the Hindu-Arabic system. .

SCIENCE & MATH

RENAISSANCE

WORD BOX

Addition	printing	equal
Greek	twenty	Medieval
Plus	eleven	Renaissance
subtraction	mathematics	fifty
Arabic	re-birth	minus
Hindu-Arabic	two	

95

Napier's Bones

John Napier
1550-1617

John Napier (1550-1617) was a Scottish nobleman who loved mathematics. He invented logarithms and developed his famous rods used for multiplication, division, and square roots of numbers. The rods were like a movable multiplication table or early slide rule, the precursor to the pocket calculator. Because the rods were often made of bone or ivory strips, they were sometimes called "Napier's Bones."

You may make a copy of Napier's Bones by copying the following strips onto lightweight cardstock (see below). Then use them to find products as illustrated below. To find 758 x 6, place the strips headed 7, 5, and 8 side by side. Place the index beside the three strips. Use the numbers that are opposite 6 on the index. Start at the right and add diagonally to find the product.

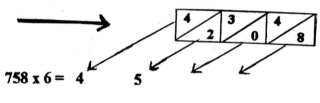

To multiply 849 x 27, place the strips headed 8, 4, and 9 side by side, and place the index beside the three strips. Use the numbers that are opposite the 2 on the index, as well as those opposite the 7. Add the numbers diagonally and regroup to the next diagonal columns if necessary. 849 x 27 = 22,923

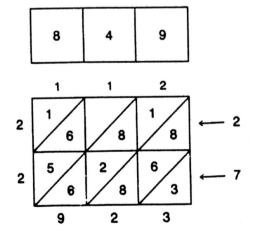

Napier's Bones

Use the ten strips of Napier's Bones to find the following products. Check your answers by multiplying.

1. 66 x 4
2. 70 x 5
3. 85 x 7
4. 54 x 3

5. 92 x 8
6. 195 x 6
7. 273 x 9
8. 58 x 7

9. 1,375 x 4
10. 2,496 x 5
11. 25 x 34
12. 571 x 62

13. 384 x 95
14. 78 x 36
15. 749 x 68

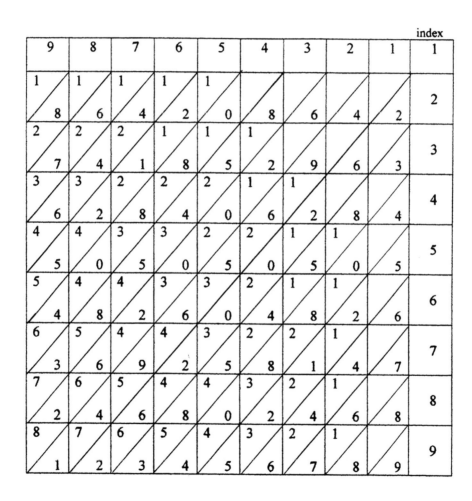

Note: You may want to include numbers with zeros. To do so, make another strip with all zeros.

Inventions

1450 – Gutenberg: moveable type and printing press

1450 – Nicholas of Cusa: concave lense for nearsighted

1500 – Peter Henleing: portable clock

1565 – Konrad von Gesner: pencil

1568 – Jacques Besson: first screw cutting lathe

1569 – Mercator: new projector or map making (cartography)

1589 – William Lee: knitting machine

1590 – Hans Jenson: compound microscope

1590 – Hans Lippershey: telescope

1592 – Galileo: thermometer

1594 – John Napier: logarithms

1622 – William Oughred: slide rule

1624 – Cornelius Drebbel: submarine

Renaissance Inventor Match

_____1. Johannes Gutenberg   A. invented the pencil

_____2. Nicholas of Cusa   B. built first screw cutting lathe

_____3. Konrad von Gesner   C. built first knitting machine

_____4. John Napier   D. designed a new projector for map making

_____5. Hans Janssen   E. invented concave lenses to correct nearsightedness

_____6. Galileo Galilei   F. perfected the technology of moveable type

_____7. Jacques Besson   G. built the first submarine

_____8. Mercator   H. invented the slide rule

_____9. William Lee   I. invented the calculator

_____10. William Oughtred   J. invented the thermometer

_____11. Wilhelm Schickard   K. compiled logarithm tables

_____12. Cornelius Drebbel   L. developed compound microscope

_____13. Peter Henlein   M. invented portable clocks

SCIENCE & MATH

answers: 1.f, 2.e, 3.a, 4.k, 5.l, 6.j, 7.b, 8.d, 9.c, 10.h, 11.i, 12.g, 13.m

Renaissance Explorers

Columbus

Though Christopher Columbus (1451-1506) was born in Genoa, Italy, he had to go to Spain to get money for his exploration plans. After Columbus convinced King Ferdinand and Queen Isabella to finance his 1492 voyage, others representing the Spanish crown soon followed, including the adventurer Cortes. The result was a huge colonial empire for the Spanish that included Mexico, Central America, Florida, much of southwestern United States, West Indies, and all of South America except Brazil.

Cortes

Hernando Cortes (1485-1547), who was born in Spain, went to the West Indies as early as 1504 when he was only 19 years old. By 1511 he had helped conquer Cuba. In 1519 he explored the east coast of Mexico and founded the settlement of Veracruz.

Cortes took his soldiers overland to the Aztec Indian capital of Tenochtitlan, which today is Mexico City. Cortes found the city to be highly developed and well-run by its leader Montezuma. Cortes was warmly welcomed by Montezuma but Cortes did not return the favor. He took Montezuma prisoner and had conquered the city by 1521.

Activities~

Complete mini-biographies for Columbus and Cortes:

Full name: _____ Full name: _____
Country of birth: _____ Country of birth: _____
Date of birth: _____ Date of birth: _____
Places explored: Places explored:

_____   _____
_____   _____

Imagine that Hernando Cortes is hiring sailors and soldiers for one of his adventures. Write an imaginary "Help Wanted" ad for him.

_____

_____

PRINCE HENRY THE NAVIGATOR

Prince Henry

In general the Italians of the Renaissance had little interest in exploring and conquering new worlds. Henry the Navigator (1394-1460), a son of King John I of Portugal, was the person who sparked European interest in exploration and geography.

Prince Henry, who never actually went on any of the voyages, set up a navigational school at Sagres on the southwest tip of Portugal. From the lookout of his fort-like school, he could watch ships, plan with sea captains, and work with cartographers as they correctly mapped the African coast as far as Sierra Leone. Prince Henry would invite scholars to the school at Sagre where they would exchange information about unknown worlds and work to perfect new navigational instruments.

Activity~

Create a brochure advertising Prince Henry's school.

Name of the school: _____

Location of school: _____

What kinds of people should come:
_____
_____

Name of the person running the school:
_____

Reference for the head of school:
_____

Activities for those attending:
_____

Draw a picture to advertise the school:

EXPLORERS

101

Columbus

Part I

Exploration, navigation, ships, and sailing captivated the imagination of young Christopher Columbus. His dream was to find a water route to the Indies, Cathay (China), and Cipanga (Japan). Prince Henry the Navigator of Portugal, whose life was devoted to training sailors and advancing knowledge of navigation, was a strong influence on Columbus.

Why search for an eastern water route to these exotic places? Columbus wanted to establish a trade route for eastern civilizations and western civilizations.

Much of the knowledge of ancient cultures had been lying dormant in books that most people did not have access to and could not read anyway. During the Renaissance people began to rediscover the great achievements of earlier centuries and to learn from them. They eventually even improved on these ideas.

What did the science of Columbus's time look like? What did they believe about the world and its geography?

Activity~

Here are some ideas that were common knowledge in Columbus' time. Use a reference book, such as an encyclopedia, to look up each name on the list. Match the idea to the person who is credited with the belief.

_____ Aristotle   a. the earth is the center of the universe and all the planets revolve around it.

_____ Ptolemy   b. thought the map drawn in ancient times by Ptolemy was correct. It showed the land between Spain and China much larger than it is and the Atlantic Ocean much smaller.

_____ Columbus   c. believed the moon was a flat disk.

EXPLORERS

Part II
Many superstitious and uneducated people during Columbus' time believed the earth was flat. Draw a picture to match their ideas.

#1 The earth can't be round. People on the underside of the world couldn't walk around upside down.

#2 The earth can't be round. Plants couldn't possibly grow because rain can't rain up!

Activity~

1) Without the benefit of our modern technology, how could the scientists of the Renaissance know that the earth was not flat? Think about it. List two or three observations that Renaissance scientists could have made to figure out that the earth was round.
2) What proof do we have in our own technological age that the earth is round? List two or three ways we have to prove the earth is round.
3) Look at a map of our modern world. Now imagine Ptolemy's map that shows the land between Spain and China as much bigger than it is and the Atlantic Ocean much smaller. Draw your version of this map. Use your imagination. You might want to look at some pictures in books of maps that were drawn in Columbus' time.

By the way, what continent did Ptolemy not know about when he drew his map? OOOPS! Well, Columbus found it didn't he!?

EXPLORERS

103

You are a Sailor with Columbus

It is early September 1492, and you are a sailor on the crew ship *Santa Maria*. It is one of three ships sailing together to discover the New World. The other two are called the *Niña* and the *Pinta*.

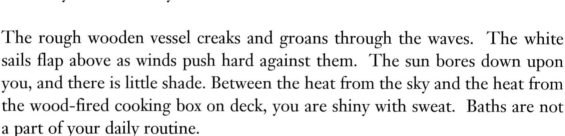

You are sailing west across the Atlantic. You left Spain two months ago and stopped at the Canary Islands to replenish supplies. That was a month ago. Since then, the crew has seen only the endless, shimmering reflection of water. It is a hot, tiring, and scary voyage because you don't really know what lies ahead in the ocean.

The rough wooden vessel creaks and groans through the waves. The white sails flap above as winds push hard against them. The sun bores down upon you, and there is little shade. Between the heat from the sky and the heat from the wood-fired cooking box on deck, you are shiny with sweat. Baths are not a part of your daily routine.

Yesterday the crew got very angry and threatened to mutiny if land was not sighted soon. Everyone agreed to search for three more days and then turn back to Spain. Your eyes stare at the far horizon for anything to see besides the straight lines of the water.

Think about what you would have seen and what sounds you would have heard during this voyage. Fill those in on the chart below. Then imagine what you would feel with your fingers, toes, and skin. Write those ideas under the touch column. What could you have tasted or smelled in that place?

EXPLORERS

See	*Hear*	*Touch*	*Smell*	*Taste*

Draw a picture of the ship with you as part of the crew.

Write a paragraph describing what it was like to be a sailor with Columbus.

I am _____

_____

_____

_____

_____

_____

_____

_____

EXPLORERS

EXPLORERS & INVENTORS

"This compass really makes sailing a breeze."
Cortes

"I sailed all around the world. Who will believe it?"
Magellan

"I thought we were going to India."
Columbus

"All I wanted to do was share my ideas about God. Now look at the trouble I've caused."
Martin Luther

"I did go to India and China. I will never understand how Columbus got so mixed up. He would have seen some amazing grey powder used in firecrackers."
Marco Polo

"A telescope can surely get a man in trouble." **Copernicus**

EXPLORERS

"I think I'll get a book printed about all these Renaissance tales."
Gutenberg

EXPLORERS AND INVENTIONS OF THE RENAISSANCE

FILL IN THE BLANK

_____ opened the door to modern astronomy. He had the "new" idea that the sun was the center of the solar system.

_____ was imported from China and changed warfare forever. Guns and cannons were better than arrows, spears, or even knights on horseback.

_____ made learning available to all by putting millions of books and tracts into print.

_____ made navigation more precise so that ships could travel farther and faster.

_____ traveled overland from Venice, Italy, to India and China.

_____ accidentally discovered the New World while searching for a shorter route from Europe to India.

_____ sailed around South America and across the Pacific Ocean to Asia. His explorations proved that the world was round.

_____ published tracts that introduced new ideas about God and humankind.

Copernicus	Ferinand Magellan
magnetic compass	Christopher Columbus
gunpowder	Marco Polo
Martin Luther	printing

RENAISSANCE IDEALS ACTIVITY

Using Renaissance words and names create acronyms that tell about the time period. Use the IDEA BOX or use your own words.

R_____
A_____
P_____
H_____
A_____
E_____
L_____

M_____
A_____
S_____
A_____
C_____
C_____
I_____
O_____

R_____
E_____
N_____
A_____
I_____
S_____
S_____
A_____
N_____
C_____
E_____

CREATE YOUR OWN
(Use only as many lines as you need.)

_____
_____
_____
_____
_____
_____
_____
_____
_____
_____
_____

Renaissance

WORD BOX

Classical	ancient	rebirth	experiments
artists	Italy	St. Peter's columns	inventions
oil paint	nature	navigator	oligarchy
explorers	Henry	medici	mythology
science	ships	sculptors	

108

Renaissance Evaluation

You have learned about artists and their artwork, inventors and their inventions, as well as famous architects and their creations. Use your productive thinking skills to choose:

1. One of my favorite inventions from this time period is the _____.

   It was invented by _____.

   It was used to _____.

2. One of my favorite paintings from this unit was _____.

   The artist who did this work was _____.

   It shows _____.

3. A work of architecture I learned about was_____.

   It is located in _____.

   Some of its features are _____.

4. A famous person from this period is _____.

   He was famous for _____.

5. If I had lived in the Renaissance time I would have been a _____ _____ and _____.

109

REVIEW

A LETTER HOME

Write a letter home describing what you saw and did in the Renaissance time period. Who were your friends? Where did you go?

Create a Renaissance
Date:_____

Dear_____,

_____

_____

_____

_____

_____

_____

Draw a picture or cartoon to illustrate your letter.

With Renaissance curiosity,

_____

110

BIBLIOGRAPHY FOR RENAISSANCE

Burns, Edward. *Western Civilizations*. Norton.

Canaday, John. *Mainstreams of Modern Art*. Holt, Rinehart, Winston.

Clark, Judith. *History of Art*. Mallard Press.

Clark, Kenneth, *Civilisation*. Harper & Row.

Cole, Bruce and Adelheid Gealt. *Art of the Western World*. Summit Books.

Dorra, Henri. *Art in Perspective*. Harcourt Brace Jovanovich.

Garder, Helen. *Art Through the Ages*. Harcourt Brace.

Hartt, Frederick. *Italian Renaissance Art*. Prentice-Hall.

Hollingsworth, Patricia and Stephen Hollingsworth. *Smart Art*. Zephyr Press.

Jacobs, Jay. *Encyclopedia of World Art*. Octopus Books.

Janson, H. W. *History of Art*. Prentice Hall.

Platt, Richard. *Smithsonian Visual Timeline of Inventions*. Dorling Kindersley.

Rienits, Rex and Thea. *Voyages of Columbus*. Crescent Books.

Steves, Rick and Gene Openshaw. *Europe 101*. John Muir Publications.

Strickland, Carol and John Boswell. *The Annotated Mona Lisa*. Universal Press.

Turvey, Peter. *Timelines Inventions*. Franklin Watts.

Wallis, Frank. *Ribbons of Time*. Weidenfeld & Nicolson.

Winters, Nathan. *Architecture is Elementary*. Gibbs Smith Publisher.

Wood, Tim. *Renaissance*. Viking.

World Book Encyclopedia